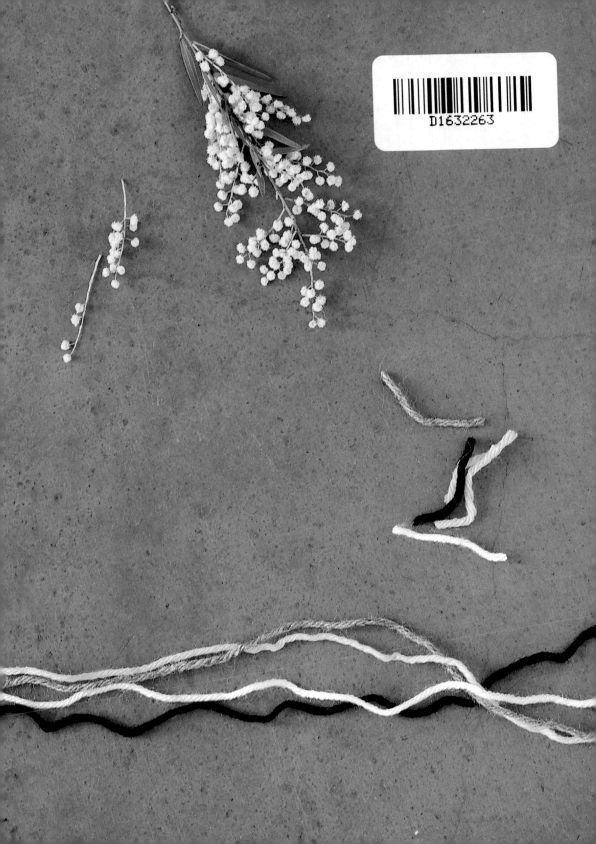

DECORATING WITH POMPOMS & TASSELS

20 CREATIVE PROJECTS

ÉMILIE GREENBERG
& KARINE THIBOULT-DEMESSENCE

Photographs: Corinne Jamet Moreno Ruiz
Stylist: Karine Thiboult-Demessence
with Émilie Greenberg

Thames & Hudson

CONTENTS

INTRODUCTION

Pompoms and tassels can add a touch of wit and creativity to any interior. They are surprisingly easy to make from many different materials, ranging from wool and paper to felt and fabric.

The twenty projects in this book include a selection of appealing decorations to adorn your home. Whether your style is rustic, quirky, boho or chic, there are tassels and pompoms to match it.

Find out how to upcycle an old t-shirt into some flouncy fridge magnets, transform a woven bag by studding it with tassels, weave fresh and fake flowers together into a garland of greenery, or add a sweet touch to a baby's bedroom with pastel pompoms. Let your imagination run free and you'll soon think up lots of new ways to put pompoms and tassels to work!

WHAT YOU NEED

Materials

Wool in a variety of types
    (mohair, angora, acrylic)
    and colours (metallic,
    neon, variegated)
Stranded embroidery yarn
Felt
Carded wool
Tissue paper
Crêpe paper
Tulle fabric
Leather
Cotton jersey
Paper raffia ribbon
Ready-made pompoms

To make the pompoms and tassels

Cardboard
Pompom maker
Scissors
Pencil
Compass
Sewing thread
Embroidery thread

For the projects

Fresh flowers, leaves and
    twigs
Bias binding
Pipecleaners
Needles
Invisible thread
String
Glue (PVA and contact)
Glue gun
Fabric dye
Wooden embroidery hoop
Wooden beads
Wooden craft dowels
Self-adhesive magnets
Blank canvases

BASIC TECHNIQUES

Making a basic pompom

Cut two identical circles, 8 cm in diameter, out of thick
cardboard. Cut a 3-cm hole out of the centre of both, and place
one on top of the other. Then make a cut through the ring into
the central hole. Tie your yarn around one end of the ring
and begin to wrap the yarn around the ring until it is well
covered with yarn. Cut a piece of yarn about 20 cm long and
slide it between the two cardboard layers at the place where
the ring is cut. Begin to cut through the wrapped yarn along
the outer edge of the ring, sliding the cut length into the
gap between the layers as you go. When you've finished cutting,
tie the length firmly in the centre. Remove the cardboard,
fluff up the yarn to form a ball and trim it into shape.

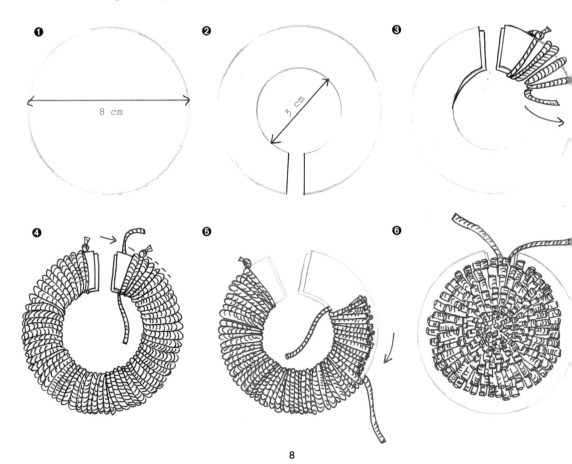

Using a pompom maker

Plastic pompom makers are easy to buy in craft shops. The pompom maker is made up of two plastic rings that are layered on top of each other, but the rings can also be separated into two halves. The method is the same as for the basic pompom, but you wrap the yarn around one half-circle at a time. When both half-circles are fully covered, snap them together. Then cut a piece of yarn as a tie and begin to cut through the outer edge of the wrapped wool, pulling the tie down into the gap between the two layers. Knot the tie firmly and remove the plastic rings before fluffing up the yarn and trimming it.

Making a basic tassel

Wrap wool or cotton yarn around a square of thick cardboard. Thread a piece of yarn between the wool and the cardboard and tie it in a knot at the top. Cut through the wrapped wool at the other end of the cardboard to free it. Tie another piece of yarn around the loose wool, about a quarter of the way down from the top. Then trim the cut ends neatly. Instructions for different types of tassel can be found on the project pages.

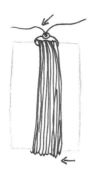 

POMPOM CUSHIONS

Level of difficulty
Double pompom: Medium
Large pompom: Easy

Time required to make one pompom
Double pompom: 10 mins
Large pompom: 5 mins

Time required to customize the cushion
30 mins

Material
Acrylic wool in black,
  grey and green
Cardboard
Compass
Scissors
Large embroidery needle
Button thread or other
  strong sewing thread
4 black buttons, 2 cm in
  diameter (1 button for
  each pompom)
Comb
Ready-made cushions
  with covers

Spruce up an old cushion by adding a burst of bright colour. Choose from a row of double pompoms in two colours or a single big one for extra impact!

To make the double pompom

1. Draw and cut out two 8-cm cardboard pompom rings, as shown on page 8.

2. Place one on top of the other and tie the black wool to one end.

3. Wrap the wool around both rings by passing it through the slit. Go around the ring 4 times, making sure the card is completely covered by wool. When you finish, tie off the ends.

4. Cut a 30-cm length of wool as a tie. Slide it between the two card layers at the place where the ring is cut.

5. Cut through the wrapped yarn along the outer edge of the ring, sliding the cut length into the gap between the layers as you go (see page 8).

6. When you've finished cutting, tie the length firmly in the centre. Remove the cardboard, fluff up the yarn to form a ball and trim.

7. Make 2 more black pompoms in the same way.

8. For the smaller grey pompoms, wrap the grey wool around three of your fingers, looping it around 50 times.

9. Slide the wrapped wool off your hand, tie a length of wool around the middle and cut through the looped ends.

POMPOM CUSHIONS

(continued)

10. Fluff up the pompom and trim as before. Make two more grey pompoms in the same way.

11. Stitch the 3 grey pompoms into the middle of the 3 black pompoms.

To make the large pompom

1. Draw and cut out two 12-cm cardboard pompom rings, as shown on page 8.

2. Using the green wool, follow the instructions for the black pompom on page 11.

3. Dip the finished pompom in warm water for 30 secs. Use a comb to untangle and fluff up the strands. Leave the pompom to dry or use a hairdryer.

To customize the cushion

1. Thread a button onto the knotted end of a double length of thread. Stitch through the centre of the cushion, leaving the button on the reverse side. Pass the needle back and forth through the cushion a few times to create a quilted effect, then bring it through to the front again.

2. Stitch through the pompom, attaching it to the front of the cushion, then pass the needle back to the reverse side again.

3. Wrap the thread around the button and tie it off. Attach the other pompoms in the same way.

TASSELLED THROW

Level of difficulty
Easy

Time required to make one tassel
10 mins

Time required to customize the throw
1 hr

Materials
1 throw
Cardboard
1 ball of yellow cotton
   yarn
Variegated grey yarn
Scissors
4 wooden beads,
   1 cm in diameter
Comb

Add a boho touch to a throw or shawl.

To make the tassels

1. Cut a 13 × 10 cm piece of cardboard.

2. Make a slit at the top and slide one end of the yellow yarn into it, to hold it in place. Wrap the yarn around the cardboard 150 times.

3. Slide two strands of grey yarn between the yellow yarn and the cardboard. Tie them firmly at one end to hold the yellow strands together. This forms the top of the tassel.

4. Cut through the yellow yarn at the opposite end to the tie. Fold the yarn in half, so the tie is at the top.

5. Tie another strand of grey yarn around the tassel, 2.5 cm down from the tie at the top.

6. Push a bead into the strands below the second knot, arranging the yarn to give the tassel volume.

7. Tie another strand of grey yarn around the tassel, just below the bead. Trim off any excess yarn.

8. Make 3 more tassels in the same way.

9. Dip the tassels in warm water for 1 min. Use a comb to smooth the strands. Leave to dry or use a hairdryer.

To customize the throw

1. Plait the tied threads at the top of each tassel neatly together.

2. Sew a tassel to each corner of the throw.

TASSELLED CUSHION

Level of difficulty
Easy

Time required to make one tassel
10 mins

Time required to customize a cushion
45 mins

Materials
1 cushion with cover
1 piece of grey leather, measuring 19 × 30 cm
Ruler
Scissors
Contact glue
Clothes pegs
Heavy duty needle
Grey cotton thread

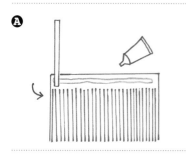

A

Tip
Before cutting the leather fringe, put masking tape over the area you don't want to cut.

Good to know
Consider investing in a rotary cutter, which is good not only for cutting leather but also fabric and paper.

Upcycle a cushion cover by adding leather tassels to its corners. Metallic leather would work particularly well for this.

To make the tassels

1. Cut out 4 leather rectangles, measuring 9 × 15 cm, and 4 thin leather strips measuring 4 × 0.5 cm.

2. Take one of the rectangles and turn it into a fringe by making a series of 5.5-cm cuts along its length, 3 mm apart.

3. Place the rectangle right side down. Take one of the thin stripes and glue its end in the top left uncut corner of the rectangle, as shown in diagram **A**, allowing a 1-cm overlap.

4. Spread glue along the uncut edge of the fringed rectangle.

5. Roll the tassel up firmly. Use a clothes peg to hold the glued end together until it dries.

6. Repeat this process to make another 3 tassels.

To customize the cushion

1. Cut open the corners of the cushion cover carefully.

2. Slide the tassels into position and stitch them in place with grey thread.

SPOTTED SEAT COVER

Level of difficulty
Difficult

**Time required to make
one felted wool pompom**
3 mins + drying time

**Time required to make
the seat cover**
8 hrs

Materials
Carded wool in black,
   yellow, white and grey
Ruler
Soap
Invisible thread
Long needle
220 cm of black bias
   binding

An old stool or chair gets a new lease
of life from this colourful cover,
made from balls of felted wool.

To make the felted wool balls

1. Unroll the batt of carded wool,
measure off a 10 cm piece of wool,
then pull it off the batt.

2. Pull gently on the sides of the wool
to thin it out and make it wispy.

3. Roll up the piece of wool carefully
to form a dense ball.

4. Dip the ball into hot soapy water.

5. Roll the felt between your palms
until it forms a dense ball, around
2 cm in diameter.

6. You will need to make 144 balls in
total, divided between each of the four
colours. Leave them to dry for at least
24 hours.

Tip
You can also buy ready-made
balls of felted wool. For
this project, choose balls
that are 2 cm in diameter.

Good to know
Carded wool is sold in
small bundles called batts.
A wide range of colours are
available, so it's easy
to come up with your own
combination of shades.

SPOTTED SEAT COVER

(continued)

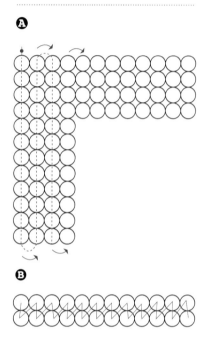

A

B

To make the seat cover

1. Thread a needle with invisible thread and knot it at one end. Pass the needle through the centre of 12 felt balls, alternating the colours of the balls, to form the first row of the design.

2. Thread on another 12 balls to make the second row. Continue making new rows until all the balls are threaded. Arrange the balls to form a square made up of 12 rows.

3. To join the horizontal rows together, cut another length of invisible thread and knot its end. Pass it through the rows vertically in a weaving motion, working down one row and up the next, as shown in diagram **A**. To make the seat cover even firmer, cut another length of thread and work in a zigzag movement across the horizontal rows, as shown in diagram **B**.

4. Cut 4 lengths of bias binding, each 55 cm long. Fold each length in half and stitch it closed to form a tie.

5. Fold the ties in two at their central point. Stitch them in position in the middle of each side of the cover or at the corners, to match the positioning of the legs on your stool or chair.

TASSELLED NAPKINS

Level of difficulty
Easy

Time required to make one tassel
3 mins

Time required to customize a napkin
15 mins

Materials
Cotton or linen napkins
Scissors
Cardboard
2 skeins of yellow
  stranded embroidery
  yarn
1 skein of grey stranded
  embroidery yarn
Comb

Matching or constrasting tassels liven up plain table napkins. You'll need to make 4 tassels for each napkin.

To make the tassels

1. Cut a piece of cardboard measuring 5 × 8 cm.

2. Make a slit at the top and slide one end of the yellow yarn into it, to hold it in place.

3. Wrap the yarn around the cardboard 20 times.

4. Slide a strand of grey yarn between the yellow yarn and the cardboard. Tie it firmly at one end to hold the yellow strands together. This forms the top of the tassel.

5. Cut through the yellow yarn at the opposite end to the tie. Fold the yarn in half, so the tie is at the top.

6. Wrap a strand of grey yarn around the tassel several times, 1 cm down from the top. Tie it firmly.

7. Make 3 more tassels in the same way.

8. Dip the tassels in warm water for 30 secs. Use a comb to smooth and fluff up the strands. Leave to dry or use a hairdryer.

To customize the napkins

Unpick the seams on the corners of the napkin. Stitch a tassel in each corner and sew the seam closed again.

Tip
You can make multicoloured tassels by combining different colours of yarn. For example, try 10 rounds of yellow thread and 10 rounds of grey thread.

POMPOM TABLECLOTH

Level of difficulty
Medium

Time required to
make one pompom
3 mins

Time required to
customize the tablecloth
6 hrs

Materials
Tablecloth
1 ball of yellow mohair
   yarn
Fork
Sewing thread
Scissors
Dressmaker's pencil or
   tailor's chalk

Yellow mohair yarn makes delightful fluffy pompoms that resemble mimosa blossoms, bringing a touch of springtime to your table.

To make a pompom

1. Tie one end of the yarn to the fork.

2. Wrap the yarn around the fork 50 times.

3. Tie a double strand of thread vertically around the wrapped yarn, passing it through the prongs of the fork.

4. Cut the loops of yarn on both sides of the fork. Fluff up the pompom and trim it into shape with the scissors.

To customize the tablecloth

1. Use the dressmaker's pencil to mark 3 rows of dots down opposite sides of the tablecloth. Space the dots 10 cm apart and stagger them as shown in the image opposite.

2. Stitch a pompom onto each of the dots. For a tablecloth 140 cm in length, you will need 94 pompoms in total (47 for each side, arranged in 3 rows of 16, 15 and 16).

Good to know
Use sewing thread to tie the mohair pompoms together. Mohair yarn is too fragile and breaks easily.

SAY IT WITH FLOWERS

Leftover odds and ends of wool and a few twigs from your local park are combined to make a pretty table decoration.

<u>Level of difficulty</u>
Easy

<u>**Time required to make one pompom**</u>
10 mins

<u>**Time required to assemble one flower**</u>
2 mins

<u>**Materials**</u>
25% wool mix yarn in
   white, pink and green
Pompom maker or
   2 cardboard pompom
   rings, 3.5 cm in
   diameter
Scissors
Glue gun
5 twigs

To make the pompoms

1. Use the pompom maker or cardboard circles to make a pompom, according to the instructions on page 8. Use a length of wool to tie the pompom together. Wrap the wool several times around the centre of the pompom and knot it firmly, then trim the ends.

2. Trim and shape the pompom to make a dense and fluffy ball.

3. Make four more pompoms in the same way.

To make the flowers

Using the glue gun, squirt a drop of glue onto the pompom, position it on the twig and push firmly. Do the same for the rest of the pompoms.

Good to know
The more layers of wool you wrap around your pompom maker, the denser and firmer your pompom will be.

TASSELLED SHOPPER BAG

Level of difficulty
Easy

**Time required to make
one tassel**
2 mins

**Time required to
customize the bag**
1½ hrs

Materials
Straw shopper bag
Embroidery needle
Scissors
Cardboard
Ruler
3 skeins of yellow
    stranded embroidery
    yarn
18 jump rings in silver
    metal
Comb
Masking tape
Yellow spray paint

Tip
This bag would also look
great with a rainbow of
coloured tassels.

This bright bag makes shopping a treat.

To make the tassels

1. Cut a piece of cardboard measuring
3 × 4 cm.

2. Make a slit at the top and slide one
end of the yellow yarn into it, to hold
it in place.

3. Wrap the yarn around the cardboard
10 times.

4. Slide a strand of yarn between the
looped yarn and the cardboard. Tie it
firmly at one end to form the top.

5. Fix a jump ring over the tie.

6. Cut through the yarn at the opposite
end to the tie and let it hang down.

7. Wrap a strand of yarn around the
tassel several times, 1 cm down from
the top. Tie it firmly.

8. Make 17 more tassels in the same way.

9. Dip the tassels in warm water for 30
secs. Use a comb to smooth the strands.
Leave to dry or use a hairdryer.

To customize the basket

1. Stick a line of masking tape around
the bag, 6 cm up from the bottom.

2. Spray paint the area below the tape,
using a back-and-forth motion.

3. When the paint is dry, peel off the
tape. Sew the tassels onto the bag
in 4 staggered rows of 5, 4, 5 and 4.
Stitch through the jump rings and
leave 7 cm gaps between tassels.

DIP-DYED TASSELS

Level of difficulty
Medium

Time required to make one tassel
12 mins + drying time

Time required to make the wall hanging
1½ hrs

Materials
1 ball of unbleached
  cotton yarn
Fabric dye in deep pink,
  green and grey
2 wooden craft dowels,
  measuring 19 cm
  and 25 cm
Cardboard
Scissors
Comb

Tassels needed
2 green, 2 pink, 1 grey

A wall hanging in graduated shades.

To make the tassels

1. Cut a piece of cardboard measuring 8 × 10 cm.

2. Slit the cardboard and slide one end of the yarn into it, to hold it in place.

3. Wrap the yarn around the cardboard 100 times.

4. Slide a 50-cm length of yarn between the yarn and the cardboard. Tie it firmly at one end. Cut through the yarn at the opposite end. Wrap another strand of yarn around the tassel several times, 1 cm down from the top. Tie it firmly.

5. Make 4 more tassels in the same way.

6. Dip the tassels in warm water for 1 min. Use a comb to smooth out the strands. Squeeze out any excess water.

7. Prepare each of the fabric dyes in a separate bowl of warm water (40°C).

8. Dip the bottom 5 cm of each tassel into the dye and leave it for 1 min.

9. Pull the tassels out so only 1 cm is still under the dye. Leave for 5 mins. Pull out completely and leave to dry.

To make the wall hanging

1. Fix 2 tassels to the 19-cm dowel by wrapping the yarn tie around it.

2. Fix 3 tassels to the 25-cm dowel.

4. Use a 25-cm length of yarn to tie the dowels together. Plait another length of yarn to form a loop at the top to hang up the finished piece.

LET THERE BE LIGHT

Level of difficulty
Easy

Time required
20 mins

Materials
1 white lampshade,
   approx. 13 cm high
   and 13 cm in diameter
30 ready-made white
   pompoms, 15 mm in
   diameter
Glue gun or a packet
   of glue dots
Pencil
Tape measure

This simple project can easily be varied: try using different colour combinations or metallic or neon pompoms for a different look.

Instructions

1. To help you to arrange the pompoms in staggered rows, start by making a grid of reference marks on the lampshade in pencil. Measure the height of the lampshade and subtract 1.5 cm for the top and bottom edges (in this case, 13 - 3 = 10 cm). Divide the remaining length by 4 (in this case, 10 ÷ 4 = 2.5 cm). Then measure around the lampshade and divide by 12 (85.2 ÷ 12 = 7.1 cm). Use these measurements to make a grid template like the one on pages 70-71 and mark the reference points on the shade.

2. Place a drop of glue on each of the points with the glue gun, or stick on a glue dot.

3. Fix a ready-made pompom on each glue dot, making sure to place a hand inside the lampshade and push outwards to stick each pompom firmly in place. Wait for the glue to dry if necessary.

MORE
DREAMING · PLANS
COFFEE · ARCHI
BRIGHTER · INTERIOR
CREATING · MEETING
& MORE 80M2

FLOWERY FRIDGE MAGNET

Level of difficulty
Easy
**Time required to
make one pompom**
5 mins
**Time required to
make one magnet**
10 mins
Materials
1 old t-shirt in thin
  cotton jersey
Felt in a colour to match
  the t-shirt, measuring
  3 × 7 cm
1 skein of stranded
  embroidery yarn in
  a colour to match
  the t-shirt
Pompom maker or
  2 cardboard pompom
  rings, 3.5 cm in
  diameter
1 self-adhesive magnet,
  25 mm in diameter
Scissors
Craft knife

**An old t-shirt can quickly be recycled
into a pretty pompom magnet for your
fridge or noticeboard.**

Instructions

1. Cut three strips of fabric
lengthways from the t-shirt,
each measuring 60 × 0.5 cm.

2. Make a pompom with them using the
pompom maker or cardboard rings. Make
sure that the fabric lies as flat as
possible: it may get twisted up easily.

3. Tie off the pompom with embroidery
yarn, knotting it firmly. Do not trim
off the ends of the thread yet. Trim
the pompom to shape.

4. Cut a circle of felt, the same size
as the self-adhesive magnet.

5. Use the craft knife to make two
parallel slits in the centre of the
felt circle, as shown in diagram **Ⓐ**.

6. Pass each of the ends of the cotton
thread around the pompom through the
slits in the felt circle. Tie in a
double knot. You will now have a pompom
with a felt circle attached underneath.

7. Peel off the self-adhesive film
on the magnet and stick it onto the
felt circle.

8. Magnets in other colours and fabrics
can be made the same way.

Ⓐ

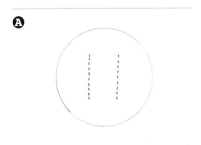

PARTY-TIME TASSELS

Level of difficulty
Easy

Time required to make one tassel
6 mins

Time required to make the garland
1¾ hrs

Materials
Plain tissue paper in
  pink and white
Polka-dot tissue paper
  in brown and green
Scissors
Ruler
String
Glue gun or PVA glue

This tissue paper garland looks good at any party, indoors or outdoors.

To make the tassels

1. Cut a sheet of tissue paper measuring 23 × 66 cm.

2. Fold it in half to make a rectangle measuring 23 × 33 cm.

3. Leave a 5-cm gap along the folded edge and cut the rest of the doubled sheet into a fringe, as shown in diagram **Ⓐ**.

4. Unfold the sheet and fold up the uncut central strip into accordeon pleats, 2 cm wide, as shown in diagram **Ⓑ**.

5. Fold the pleated paper into an inverted U-shape, as shown in diagram **Ⓒ**. Paste a narrow strip of tissue just below the top, so that the tassel holds its shape.

6. Make 15 more tassels in the same way, so you end up with 4 of each colour.

To make the garland

Thread the string through the loops at the top of the tassels, alternating the colours as you go.

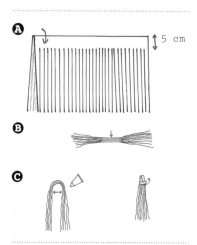

Ⓐ ↕ 5 cm

Ⓑ

Ⓒ

Tip
Consider investing in a glue gun: they give you precise control and are quite cheap.

POMPOM RUG

Level of difficulty
Medium

**Time required to make
one pompom**
4 mins

**Time required to make
the rug**
5½ hrs

Materials
5 balls of white acrylic
    yarn
5 balls of grey acrylic
    yarn
5 balls of black acrylic
    yarn
5 balls of yellow acrylic
    yarn
Cardboard
Pencil
Compass
Scissors
1 mat made of non-slip
    mesh, measuring
    50 × 70 cm

Tip
Make sure the pompoms are
packed closely together
to hide the non-slip
mat underneath.

Good to know
Low-cost acrylic wool
is best for this project.

This colourful rug would look good
by a bedside or in a living room. Use
bold contrasting tones, or try mixing
different shades of the same colour.

To make the pompoms

1. Draw and cut out two 8-cm cardboard
pompom rings, as shown on page 8.

2. Place one on top of the other and
tie the ends of all 4 shades of yarn
to one end.

3. Go around the ring 4 times, wrapping
each yarn in turn and creating an
even mix of colours. Make sure the
card is densely covered in wool. When
you finish, tie off the ends of all
4 colours.

4. Cut a 30-cm length of yarn (of any
colour) as a tie. Slide it between the
two card layers at the place where the
ring is cut.

5. Cut through the wrapped yarn along
the outer edge of the ring, sliding
the cut length into the gap between
the layers as you go (see page 8).

6. When you've finished cutting,
tie the length firmly in the centre.
Remove the cardboard and fluff up the
yarn to form a ball. Trim the pompom
to shape but do not cut the long tie
around the centre.

7. You will need to make 70 pompoms
in total.

POMPOM RUG

(continued)

To make the rug

1. Use the strand of yarn hanging from each pompom to fix it to the non-slip mat, threading it through the grid of holes and knotting it firmly. Begin with a row of 7 pompoms along one of the short edges of the mat.

2. Continue knotting until you've covered the mat with 10 rows of 7 pompoms each.

3. Turn the rug over and trim off any excess strands of yarn.

PAPER ROSES

Level of difficulty
Medium

Time required to make one pompom
15 mins

Time required to make the curtain
2½ hrs

Materials
2 packs of black crêpe
  paper
2 packs of grey crêpe
  paper
5 wooden beads,
  3 cm in diameter
Variegated grey yarn
Scissors
Glue gun
Embroidery needle
Embroidery thread in
  black and grey
1 small bowl, around
  9 cm in diameter
Chalk
1 bamboo cane,
  150 cm long
Drawing pins

Ideal for hanging between two rooms or simply as a wall decoration, this striking curtain is made from crêpe paper pompoms.

To make the paper pompoms

1. Fold a sheet of black crepe paper 10 times to form accordeon pleats, 10 cm wide.

2. Use the bowl as a template to draw 5 circles on the folded paper, as shown in diagram **Ⓐ**.

3. Cut out the 5 circles one by one, making sure to cut through all the layers of paper.

4. Using a knotted thread, stitch through the centre of each pile of 10 circles to fix them together, as shown in diagram **Ⓑ**.

5. Working from the centre of the pompom outwards, pinch 5 of the circles towards the left and 5 towards the right, as shown in diagram **Ⓒ**.

6. In the same way, make a total of 18 black pompoms and 17 grey pompoms.

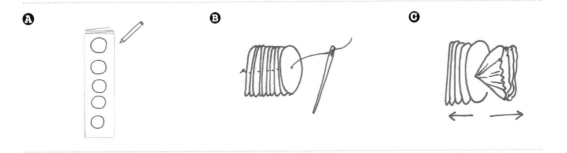

PAPER ROSES
(continued)

To make the curtain

1. Cut 5 strands of yarn, each 180 cm long, and tie one end of them around the bamboo cane.

2. Use the glue gun to stick 7 pompoms along each of the strands, spacing them about 13 cm apart and alternating the two colours.

3. Thread a wooden bead onto the bottom end of each length of yarn. Tie it in a knot and fix it with a spot of glue.

4. Use more yarn and drawing pins to hang the cane from a doorframe, wall or ceiling.

Good to know
This design would also look good in pastel shades.

POMPOM MOBILE

Level of difficulty
Difficult

Time required to make one pompom
10 mins

Time required to make the mobile
2½ hrs

Materials
50 × 45 cm of thick
   cream felt
60 × 45 cm of thick
   black felt
142 cm of black cotton
   cord
4 wooden beads,
   3 cm in diameter
1 embroidery hoop,
   20 cm in diameter
Scissors
Compass
Embroidery needle
Embroidery thread in
   black and cream
Glue gun

The subtle colours of these felt flowers look rather elegant, but the same design in bright colours would suit a child's bedroom.

To make the pompoms

1. Cut out 9 circles of black felt, measuring 10 cm in diameter.

2. Take one of these circles, fold it in half and then in half again, as shown in diagram **Ⓐ**. Position it on top of another circle of felt (the base circle) and stitch its folded corner into the centre of the base circle, as shown in diagram **Ⓑ**.

3. Fold and stitch another 3 felt circles into place on the base circle in the same way, positioning them as shown below.

4. Turn the base circle over. Fold the 4 remaining circles and stitch them to the base in the same way. The base now forms the centre of the pompom.

Ⓐ

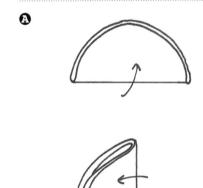

Ⓑ

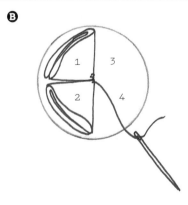

POMPOM MOBILE

(continued)

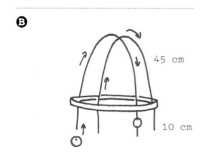

B

45 cm

10 cm

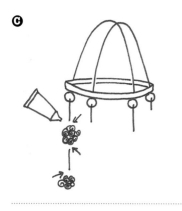

C

5. For each pompom, you will need to cut 9 felt circles of the same diameter and colour. Follow the instructions on page 47 to make 9 pompoms in total, of the following colours and diameters:

- 4 black pompoms: 9 cm, 7 cm, 5 cm, 4 cm
- 5 cream pompoms: 9 cm, 7 cm, 5 cm × 2, 4 cm

To make the mobile

1. Cut two 65-cm lengths of cotton cord to use for hanging.

2. Fix the strings between the two rings of the embroidery hoop, as shown in diagram **B**, making a loop of 45 cm over the top of the hoop and allowing 10 cm to drop below the hoop on both sides.

3. Thread a wooden bead over each of the 4 lengths of cord hanging below the hoop, and glue it into place.

4. Glue a medium pompom to the ends of 2 of the cords, as shown in diagram **C**.

5. Cut the ends of the other 2 cords to a length of 3 cm below the wooden bead. Glue 2 large pompoms to their ends.

6. Cut 5 more pieces of cord, 2 measuring 10 cm, 2 measuring 7 cm and 1 measuring 5 cm.

7. Glue the rest of the strings and pompoms in place, using the photograph on page 46 for reference.

8. Use the crossed cords at the top to hang up the mobile.

GARLAND OF GREENERY

Level of difficulty
Easy

**Time required to make
one pompom**
20 mins

Number of pompoms needed
3 medium + 6 small

Assembly time for garland
15 mins

Garland size
30 cm in diameter

Materials
1 ball of paper raffia
   ribbon in each of
   4 colours: white,
   pink, yellow and grey
Skeins of stranded
   embroidery yarn in
   white, pink, yellow
   and grey
Pompom maker or
   cardboard pompom
   rings: 2 measuring
   3.5 cm in diameter
   (for small pompoms)
   and 2 measuring 5.5 cm
   in diameter (for
   medium pompoms)
Scissors
1 bunch of eucalyptus
   leaves
1 bunch of white daisy
   chrysanthemums
1 bunch of gypsophila
   (baby's breath)
Reel of florist's wire
Cutting pliers

**This garland combines fresh and
pompom flowers to create a pretty
effect. As it dries, the eucalyptus
will turn a silvery colour.**

To make the pompoms

1. Cut the lengths of paper raffia
ribbon you need for a medium or small
pompom (see overleaf). Carefully
unravel each length of ribbon so that
the paper is flattened out.

2. Make the pompom by wrapping the
unravelled ribbon around the pompom
rings, making sure to keep it lying
as flat as possible. Tie the pompom
together using a length of embroidery
yarn in a matching colour, knotting
it firmly. Do not cut off the excess
length of thread.

3. Trim the pompom to neaten it and
fluff out the strands.

4. Repeat this process to make all
the pompoms you need:

- Medium pompoms: 3 white, 1 pink,
  1 yellow, 1 grey
- Small pompoms: 1 pink, 1 yellow,
  2 grey

To make the garland

1. Use a 95-cm length of florist's wire
to make a double circle. Close it by
twisting the ends together.

2. Trim the eucalyptus if needed,
making sure to leave a short length
of stem.

GARLAND OF GREENERY

(continued)

Raffia lengths required

For a medium pompom
  (5.5 cm in diameter),
  you will need: 3.20 m
  of raffia ribbon:
  4 × 60-cm strips +
  2 × 40-cm strips
For a small pompom
  (3.5 cm in diameter),
  you will need 1.80 m
  of raffia ribbon:
  2 × 60-cm strips +
  2 × 30-cm strips

3. Use short lengths of florist's wire to fix the eucalyptus all around the circle, covering the wire. Keep working until you're happy with the overall shape. The results will look more elegant if you position all the stems facing the same way.

4. Use the hanging lengths of embroidery yarn to fix the pompoms to the garland.

5. Use short lengths of florist's wire to fix the fresh flowers in place on the garland.

6. For best results, turn the garland around as you work to make sure that the whole ring is evenly covered and the flowers and pompoms are arranged in a well-balanced way.

THE BIGGEST BLOOMS

Level of difficulty
Easy

**Time required to
make one pompom**
10 mins

**Time required
for unfolding**
10 mins

Number of pompoms needed
4 large, 2 medium,
  3 small

Materials
Packs of tissue paper
  (1 yellow, 1 silver,
  4 white, 2 black)
  in 50 × 75 cm sheets
Craft wire
Scissors
String for hanging
Drawing pins for fixing
Ruler

Pompom paper sizes
Large: 50 × 75 cm
  (the size of sheets
  in the pack)
Medium: 37.5 × 50 cm
  (cut the large sheets
  in half)
Small: 37.5 × 25 cm
  (cut the large sheets
  into quarters)

When hung from the ceiling, these
oversized tissue-paper pompoms make
an eye-catching feature for any room.

To make the pompoms

1. Unfold the tissue paper but leave
the sheets lying on top of each other.

2. Fold the tissue paper accordeon-
style, making the pleats about 4 cm
wide (use the ruler to measure them).
Press down firmly to make sure that
the folds are sharp.

3. Fold the pleated paper in two
lengthways to make a fan shape.
Wrap a piece of craft wire around
the central fold to hold it in place.
Tie a length of string to the wire;
this will be used to hang the finished
pompom from the ceiling.

4. Cut the ends of the pleated paper
into a rounded shape. This will give
the final pompom a petal-like look.
You could also create other effects by
cutting the pleated ends into different
shapes - pointed, squared, fringed -
or by using pinking shears.

THE BIGGEST BLOOMS

(continued)

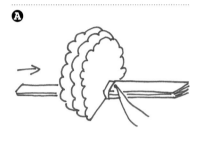

A

5. Now begin unfolding the layers of tissue. This is a delicate stage, so take your time. Lift up one layer of tissue at a time from the pleated bundle and gently pull it upwards and towards the centre, as shown in diagram **A**.

6. When all the layers on one side have been unfolded, turn the bundle around and do the same with the other side.

7. Fluff up the pompom, making sure the petals look even and attractive.

To hang the decorations

Use drawing pins to fix the strings to the ceiling. Make the strings different lengths to create a balanced effect. The flowers would look good above a bed, or perhaps over a table or sofa. You could also combine the pompom flowers with paper lanterns or balloons.

Good to know
If you're using metallic foil tissue, make sure all the sheets are positioned with the shiny side facing the same way.

Tip
For a different look, try using a mixture of plain and printed tissue paper in the same pompom.

CRIB CANOPY

Level of difficulty
Easy

**Time required to
make one pompom**
10 mins

**Time required to
make the canopy**
15 mins

Materials
Tulle fabric (2.8 m wide)
   in white, peach, pale
   green and silver grey
Pompom maker or
   cardboard pompom
   rings: 2 measuring
   3.5 cm in diameter
   (for small pompoms),
   2 measuring 5.5 cm
   in diameter (for
   medium pompoms) and
   2 measuring 9 cm in
   diameter (for large
   pompoms)
1 skein of white stranded
   embroidery yarn (in
   10 lengths of 1.30 m)
Wool needle
Scissors
White crib canopy

Tip
After you've wrapped the
fabric around the pompom
rings, push a wooden spoon
handle or pencil through
the hole in the middle
(if there's still one there)
before you begin to cut
around the edge. This will
help to hold the fabric in
place while you cut it and
push the yarn between the
rings to tie it.

Make a baby's bedroom look delightful
with this customized canopy, dotted
with pastel pompoms.

To make the pompoms

1. Cut the tulle into strips, 3 cm wide.
The total length of strips that you
will need for each pompom will vary
according to its size:

- 9.6 m for a large pompom
- 4.8 m for a medium pompom
- 2.4 m for a small pompom

2. Make the pompoms by rolling the
strips of tulle around the pompom maker
or cardboard rings as you usually would
with yarn. When you are cutting the
fabric around the edge of the circle,
slide a length of white embroidery
thread between the two circles and tie
it firmly with several knots. Cut off
any excess thread.

3. Repeat this process to make the rest
of the pompoms. A list of the sizes and
colours you need can be found overleaf.

CRIB CANOPY
(continued)

Number of pompoms needed

For each side of the
    canopy, you will need
    to make 18 pompoms,
    as follows.
Green pompoms: 2 small
    and 2 medium
White pompoms: 2 small
    and 5 large
Grey pompoms: 2 small
    and 3 medium
Peach pompoms: 2 small

To assemble the canopy

1. Cut a 1.30-m length of cotton thread
and knot it at one end.

2. Thread the needle onto the knotted
cotton and pass it through the first
pompom, sliding it down to the end of
the thread. The pompom should be held
in place by the knot.

3. Tie another knot 10 cm above the
first pompom, then thread on the next
pompom. Continue in this way until
you've filled the first thread, as
shown in diagram **A**.

4. Fill the next four threads in the
same way. Repeat these four steps if
you're planning to cover two sides
of the canopy.

5. Stitch the threaded pompoms onto
the canopy, letting the pompoms hang
at different heights to create an
attractive effect. Cover one side
first, then the other.

A

POMPOM ALPHABET

Level of difficulty
Easy
Time required
20 mins
Materials
1 bag of assorted
   ready-made pompoms
   in a range of colours
   and sizes
1 blank canvas,
   A4 size or similar
Glue gun
Pencil
Ruler

These pompom initials would liven up any child's bedroom. A version in pastel colours might make an excellent baby gift.

Instructions

1. Use the ruler and pencil to draw the rough shape of your chosen letter on the blank canvas.

2. Before you stick them down, arrange the pompoms on the canvas, aiming to create a good balance of colours and sizes. It's a good idea to place the biggest pompoms at the intersections and ends of the letter strokes, then use the smaller ones to fill in the rest of the spaces.

3. When you're happy with your design, take a photo of it for reference or make a sketch on a piece of paper, so you will remember where each pompom should go. Take the pompoms off the canvas and put them to one side.

POMPOM ALPHABET

(continued)

To assemble the picture

1. Make sure you have the photo of your design or your reference sketch to hand.

2. Apply a dot of glue to a pompom with the glue gun, and press it into position. The glue will dry quickly, so work fast. Don't worry about any strings of excess glue: you can trim these off later.

3. Keep sticking pompoms in place until the design is complete.

4. If need be, trim off any strands of dried glue.

Good to know
You could use the same technique to make pompom Space Invader motifs for an older child's room.

Tip
Use an extra-large canvas and more pompoms to spell out a whole name.

A STAR IS BORN

Level of difficulty
Easy

**Time required to
make one pompom**
2 mins

**Time required to
make one star**
5 mins

**Materials (for one
decoration)**
1 ball of silver or black
   metallic yarn
Scissors
Fork
White pipecleaner,
   30 cm long

**Made from twinkling metallic yarn,
these pompom hangings make lovely
Christmas decorations.**

To make the pompoms

1. Tie one end of the yarn to the fork.
Wrap it around the fork until the
looped yarn is around 1.5 cm thick.

2. Cut a strand of matching yarn,
60 cm long, and fold it in half.

3. Tie the double strand of thread
vertically around the wrapped
yarn, passing it through the prongs
of the fork. Repeat this process
twice more.

4. Take the tied bundle of yarn off
the fork and cut through the loops
on both sides. Be careful not to cut
the long ends of the central tie.

5. Fluff up the pompom and trim it
into shape with the scissors.

Tip
To make a two-colour
decoration, use a mixture
of silver and black yarn to
make the pompom. Wrap the
star in silver yarn first,
then add some black. Use
silver again to close the
star and hang it up.

A STAR IS BORN

(continued)

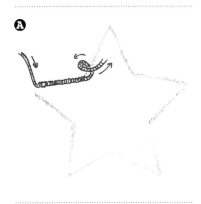

To make the star

1. Take a pipecleaner and bend it into the shape of a five-pointed star. You could copy the template from page 71, or shape the pipecleaner around a star-shaped cookie cutter if you have one. Do not join the two ends of the pipecleaner together.

2. Wrap the yarn around the star, starting at one end and taking care to cover the pipecleaner completely, as shown in diagram **A**. When you reach the other end, tie the ends of yarn together in a firm knot to close up the star.

To assemble the decoration

Use the long length of yarn used to tie the pompom together to attach the pompom to the star. Make sure the pompom is centred neatly inside the star. Use the ends or another length of yarn to make a loop to hang the decoration up.

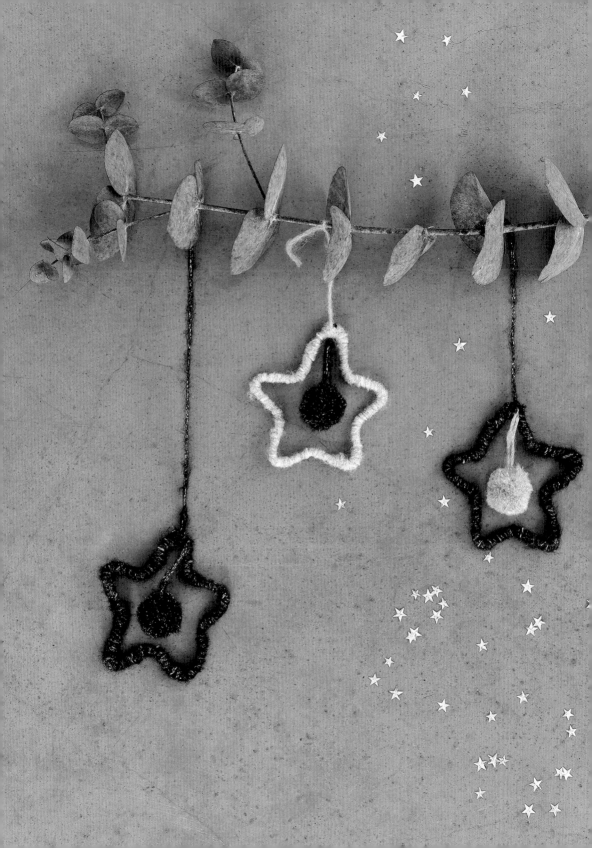

TEMPLATES

Crib canopy (page 59)

Flowery fridge magnet
(page 35)

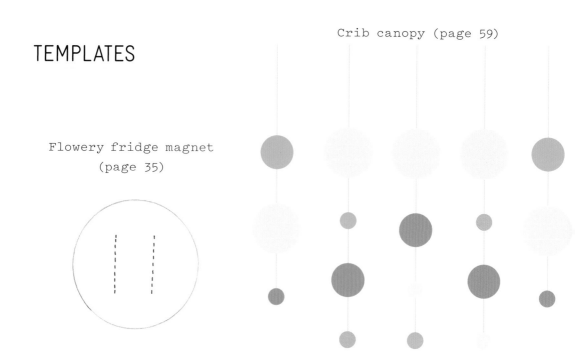

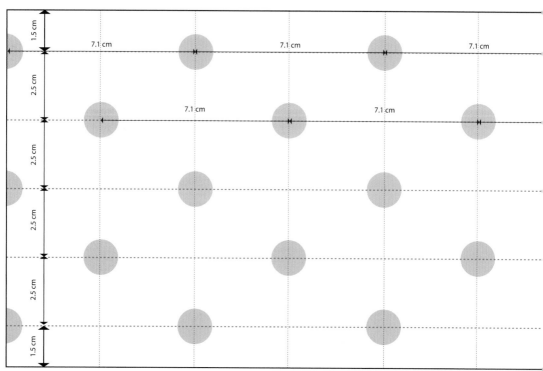

Let there be light (page 32)

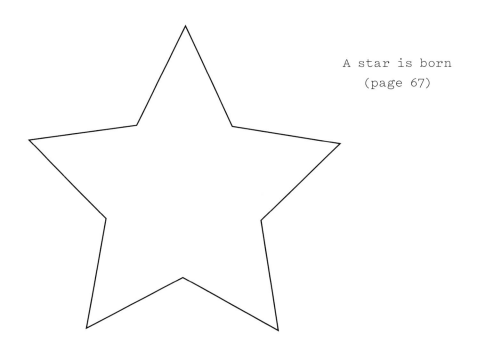

A star is born
(page 67)

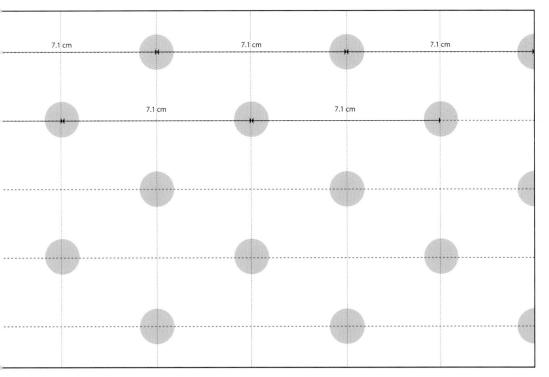

ACKNOWLEDGMENTS

We would like to thank all the companies that supplied us with materials for the projects in this book:

Wools by Phildar: Charly (cushion, page 11; rug, page 39), Strass Light (star decorations, page 67), Partner 3,5 (flowers, page 27).
Wooden beads, pipecleaners, ready-made pompoms, magnets, felt, raffia yarn, craft wire, blank canvases: Creavea.com.
Leather, binding, invisible thread, heavy felt fabric: mapetitemercerie.com.
Tulle fabric: les-coupons-de-saint-pierre.fr.
Crêpe paper and tissue paper: Clairefontaine.
Embroidery yarns and hoop: Boutique Modes & Travaux (75009).
Spray paint: Edding.com.
Fabric dye: Coloria.
Ready-made felted wool balls: Perlesandco.com.
Wooden dowels: Himmeli.fr.
Sheep print fabric (cushion, page 16): franceduvalstalla.com
Fabric (napkins, page 35): linnamorata.com

Other suppliers

Lamp: Merci.
Scissors: Botaniqueeditions.com.
Sneakers: Bensimon.
Black basket and postcards: Boutiquelesfleurs.com.
Bottle vases: Modernconfetti.com.
Macarons: Ladurée.

Translated from the French
Les petits ateliers Hachette: Des pompons dans ma déco

First published in the United Kingdom in 2016 by
Thames & Hudson Ltd, 181A High Holborn, London WC1V 7QX

Original edition © 2015 Hachette Livre (Hachette Pratique), Paris
This edition © 2016 Thames & Hudson Ltd, London

British Library Cataloguing-in-Publication Data
A catalogue record for this book is available from the British Library

ISBN 978-0-500-51890-8

Printed in Spain

To find out about all our publications, please visit **www.thamesandhudson.com**.
There you can subscribe to our e-newsletter, browse or download our current catalogue,
and buy any titles that are in print.

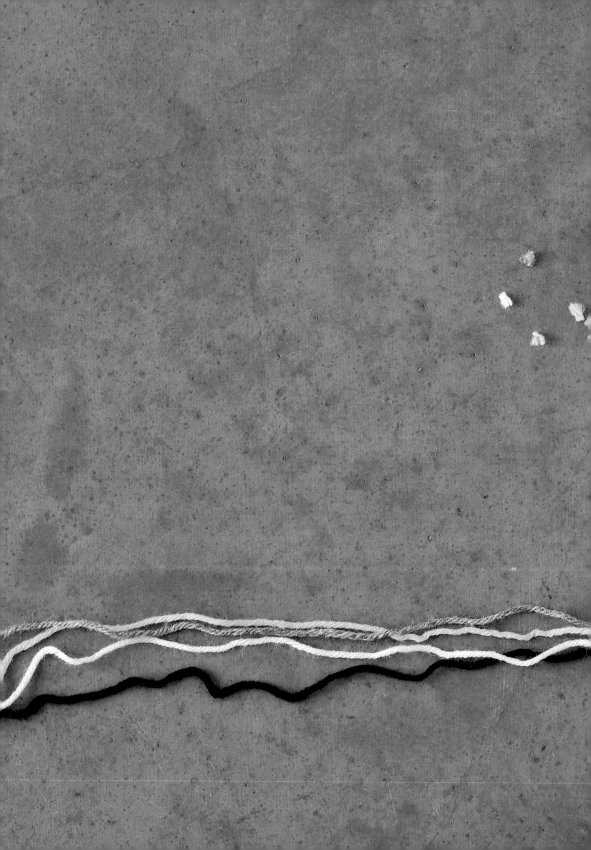